To the Zoo

Written by Lisa Harkrader
Illustrated by Susan Calitri
Cover illustrated by Mark Chambers

ISBN-13: 978-1-4127-9178-6
ISBN-10: 1-4127-9178-2

8 7 6 5 4 3 2 1

publications international, ltd.

My name is Rose. I'm a zookeeper.

As a zookeeper, my job is to take care of the animals at my zoo. I keep the animals safe, healthy, well fed, and as happy as possible.

I go to work early in the morning. I begin taking care of the animals before the zoo opens for the day.

First I check the animals and make sure they are healthy. I watch them to make sure their behavior hasn't changed. If an animal starts acting differently than usual, it may be a sign that the animal is sick.

Elephants have sensitive skin. I check the elephants for cuts and scratches. I check their feet for cracks and embedded rocks.

At my zoo, the animals live in habitats similar to their habitats in the wild. We don't want them to feel like they are in cages.

Lions, zebras, and giraffes need wide-open, grassy spaces. Birds need trees and lots of room to fly.

Tigers like to live and hunt by themselves. Gorillas, elephants, and lions live in family groups.

I prepare food for many of the animals. I feed each animal the kind of food it would eat in the wild. Lions and tigers eat meat. Rattlesnakes eat meat, too, but their meat is much smaller. Grizzly bears eat meat, but they also eat berries and nuts. Gorillas eat plants and berries. Koalas like to eat only one thing—eucalyptus leaves.

Some animals, like giraffes and elephants, have both indoor and outdoor living areas. The indoor areas keep them safe at night or comfortable when it becomes too cold or too hot for them to go outside.

Every day I must clean their indoor and outdoor living areas. I make sure they are healthy places for the animals to live.

The people who visit our zoo want to know more about the animals. I make sure the animal exhibits have lots of information for people to read.

I also put on programs to show people how different animals eat, live, and behave. I train the animals to make sure the programs are safe for both the animals and the zoo visitors.

I love the animals I take care of, but I try not to intrude upon their lives any more than I have to. I try to let them live the way they would live in the wild.

It is best if animals are raised by their mothers and fathers. They learn important things that way. But sometimes I have to raise a baby that has lost its mother and father.

I like taking care of animals.
Many animals, such as Asian wild
horses, are endangered species.
They are in danger of becoming
extinct. Zoos help all animals
live long and happy lives.